STRIVE

STRIVE

Other Books by Raphael Sidelman:

The Way to the Way

Think about it…

The Official Study Guide for the Test Called Life

The Science of Fiction (written under the pen name "Gyve Buskin")

Perspicacious Press

Tehran - Hanoi - Illisheim - Nagasaki - Kabul

I want to fly, but I have no wings.

I want to seek what's right, but I have no map.

I want to heal the sick, but I've got a cold.

I want to save those who are drowning, but I can barely swim.

I want to demand justice, but that would be criminal.

I want to sing the gospel, but I have no voice.

I want to carry the world, but I can barely stand.

I want to spread the light, but I'm in the dark.

I want to free the captive, but I'm imprisoned.

I want to tear down the wall, but there are so many bricks

I don't know where to start.

Follow the directions given herein and, surely, the only thing you will not succeed at is failure.

What does it mean to Strive?

To labor hard.

To put forth much effort.

Strive to be

Someone whose resolve is indissoluble, yet infinitely able to adapt.

What does it mean to Strive?

To labor hard.

To put forth much effort.

Strive to be

Someone whose desire is tempered by patience, reason, and an appreciation for what you already actually have.

What does it mean to Strive?

To labor hard.

To put forth much effort.

Strive to be

Someone whose judgment remains at all times within the boundaries of fact, logic, and accountability.

What does it mean to Strive?

To labor hard.

To put forth much effort.

Strive to be

Someone whose ability to accurately discern and accurately connect is never limited by an inability to listen.

What does it mean to Strive?

To labor hard.

To put forth much effort.

Strive to be

Someone who understands that attention is never paid. It is invested.

What does it mean to Strive?

To labor hard.

To put forth much effort.

Strive to be

Someone who sees that all things are varied expressions of the same source - all running their course according to the law that governs their coming and going.

What does it mean to Strive?

To labor hard.

To put forth much effort.

Strive to be

Someone with a constant awareness of the fact that, if one continually puts certain components into the soil, soon that soil will only support the growth of that which thrives on those components.

What does it mean to Strive?

To labor hard.

To put forth much effort.

Strive to be

Someone who understands that exercisable rights are merely the fruit of ongoing duty.

What does it mean to Strive?

To labor hard.

To put forth much effort.

Strive to be

Someone who never substitutes complaints for action, or action for thought.

What does it mean to Strive?

To labor hard.

To put forth much effort.

Strive to be

Someone who helps others to at least the extent that they are willing to help themselves.

What does it mean to Strive?

To labor hard.

To put forth much effort.

Strive to be

Someone who upholds values that are based upon personal insight and that are in accord with the virtues of balance and self-worth.

What does it mean to Strive?

To labor hard.

To put forth much effort.

Strive to be

Someone whose patience is never exceeded by, or exceeding, reason.

What does it mean to Strive?

To labor hard.

To put forth much effort.

Strive to be

Someone who recognizes that their success is limited only by the actuality of the laws that govern such endeavor.

What does it mean to Strive?

To labor hard.

To put forth much effort.

Strive to be

Someone who realizes that goals are not accomplished in a single, lightning stroke.

What does it mean to Strive?

To labor hard.

To put forth much effort.

Strive to be

Someone whose fascination is not limited to past experience or the ideas of others.

What does it mean to Strive?

To labor hard.

To put forth much effort.

Strive to be

Someone whose skill, ability, and ambition are not dependent on the encouragement of others.

What does it mean to Strive?

To labor hard.

To put forth much effort.

Strive to be

Someone whose every reaction is the result of habitual positive reinforcement.

What does it mean to Strive?

To labor hard.

To put forth much effort.

Strive to be

Someone who sees setback merely as a result of incomplete awareness.

What does it mean to Strive?

To labor hard.

To put forth much effort.

Strive to be

Someone to whom pain and loss are catalysts for understanding and transcendence.

What does it mean to Strive?

To labor hard.

To put forth much effort.

Strive to be

Someone who sees all challenges as opportunities for growth and improvement.

What does it mean to Strive?

To labor hard.

To put forth much effort.

Strive to be

Someone who is happy for, and inspired and encouraged by, the success of others.

What does it mean to Strive?

To labor hard.

To put forth much effort.

Strive to be

Someone whose list of achievements has no omission based on fear, incompetence, or complacency.

What does it mean to Strive?

To labor hard.

To put forth much effort.

Strive to be

Someone with an awareness that transcends your present situation, while being fully present

What does it mean to Strive?

To labor hard.

To put forth much effort.

Strive to be

Someone who sees a reason for joy and appreciation in all situations.

What does it mean to Strive?

To labor hard.

To put forth much effort.

Strive to be

Someone with the vision to see the structure, and thus the limits, of what others perceive only as obstacles.

What does it mean to Strive?

To labor hard.

To put forth much effort.

Strive to be

Someone who understands competence regarding any endeavor to be a matter of conscious awareness and persistent, positive reinforcement.

What does it mean to Strive?

To labor hard.

To put forth much effort.

Strive to be

Someone who sees creativity as your only limit.

What does it mean to Strive?

To labor hard.

To put forth much effort.

Strive to be

Someone who realizes that fantasy is an actual aspect of reality and that it merely currently lacks the foundation required to exist in the physical realm.

What does it mean to Strive?

To labor hard.

To put forth much effort.

Strive to be

Someone for whom solitude is the frequent occurrence of time spent with your best friend and trusted advisor.

What does it mean to Strive?

To labor hard.

To put forth much effort.

Strive to be

Worthy of respect and trust in all manner of interaction.

What does it mean to Strive?

To labor hard.

To put forth much effort.

Strive to be

Someone whose ability to oppose another, in any regard, is considered by all beings to be superior yet fair.

What does it mean to Strive?

To labor hard.

To put forth much effort.

Strive to be

Someone whose ability to love and accept is not limited by fear, hatred, jealousy, or perspective.

What does it mean to Strive?

To labor hard.

To put forth much effort.

Strive to be

Someone who has the courage to act rationally in all situations.

What does it mean to Strive?

To labor hard.

To put forth much effort.

Strive to be

Someone who embodies balance at all times, in all situations.

What does it mean to Strive?

To labor hard.

To put forth much effort.

Strive to be

Someone whose beliefs are eternally regarded by all honest, serious thinkers as properly conceived.

What does it mean to Strive?

To labor hard.

To put forth much effort.

Strive to be

Someone who produces more environmentally beneficial resources than you consume.

What does it mean to Strive?

To labor hard.

To put forth much effort.

Strive to be

Someone whose friendship and acquaintance is considered an honor by all who know of you.

What does it mean to Strive?

To labor hard.

To put forth much effort.

Strive to be

Someone for whom every act of giving is rooted in strength, not weakness.

What does it mean to Strive?

To labor hard.

To put forth much effort.

Strive to be

Someone who can perceive of every possible existence and still desire your own.

STRIVE

The following pages are copies of what you have just read. Consider the effects of your removing them and placing them where you will repeatedly see them as you go about your day.

What does it mean to Strive?

To labor hard.

To put forth much effort.

Strive to be

Someone whose resolve is indissoluble, yet infinitely able to adapt.

Strive to be

Someone whose desire is tempered by patience, reason, and an appreciation for what you already actually have.

Strive to be

Someone whose judgment remains at all times within the boundaries of fact, logic, and accountability.

Strive to

all times within the boundaries of fact,

Strive to be

Someone whose ability to accurately discern and accurately connect is never limited by an inability to listen.

Strive to be

Someone who understands that attention is never paid. It is invested.

Strive to be

Someone who sees that all things are varied expressions of the same source - all running their course according to the law that governs their coming and going.

Strive to be

Someone with a constant awareness of the fact that, if one continually puts certain components into the soil, soon that soil will only support the growth of that which thrives on those components.

Strive to be

Someone who understands that exercisable rights are merely the fruit of ongoing duty.

Strive to be

Someone who never substitutes complaints for action, or action for thought.

Strive to be

Someone who helps others to at least the extent that they are willing to help themselves.

Strive to be

Someone who upholds values that are based upon personal insight and that are in accord with the virtues of balance and self-worth.

Strive to be

Someone whose patience is never exceeded by, or exceeding, reason.

Strive to be

Someone who recognizes that their success is limited only by the actuality of the laws that govern such endeavor.

Strive to be

Someone who realizes that goals are not accomplished in a single, lightning stroke.

Strive to be

Someone whose fascination is not limited to past experience or the ideas of others.

Strive to be

Someone whose skill, ability, and ambition are not dependent on the encouragement of others.

Strive to be

Someone whose every reaction is the result of habitual positive reinforcement.

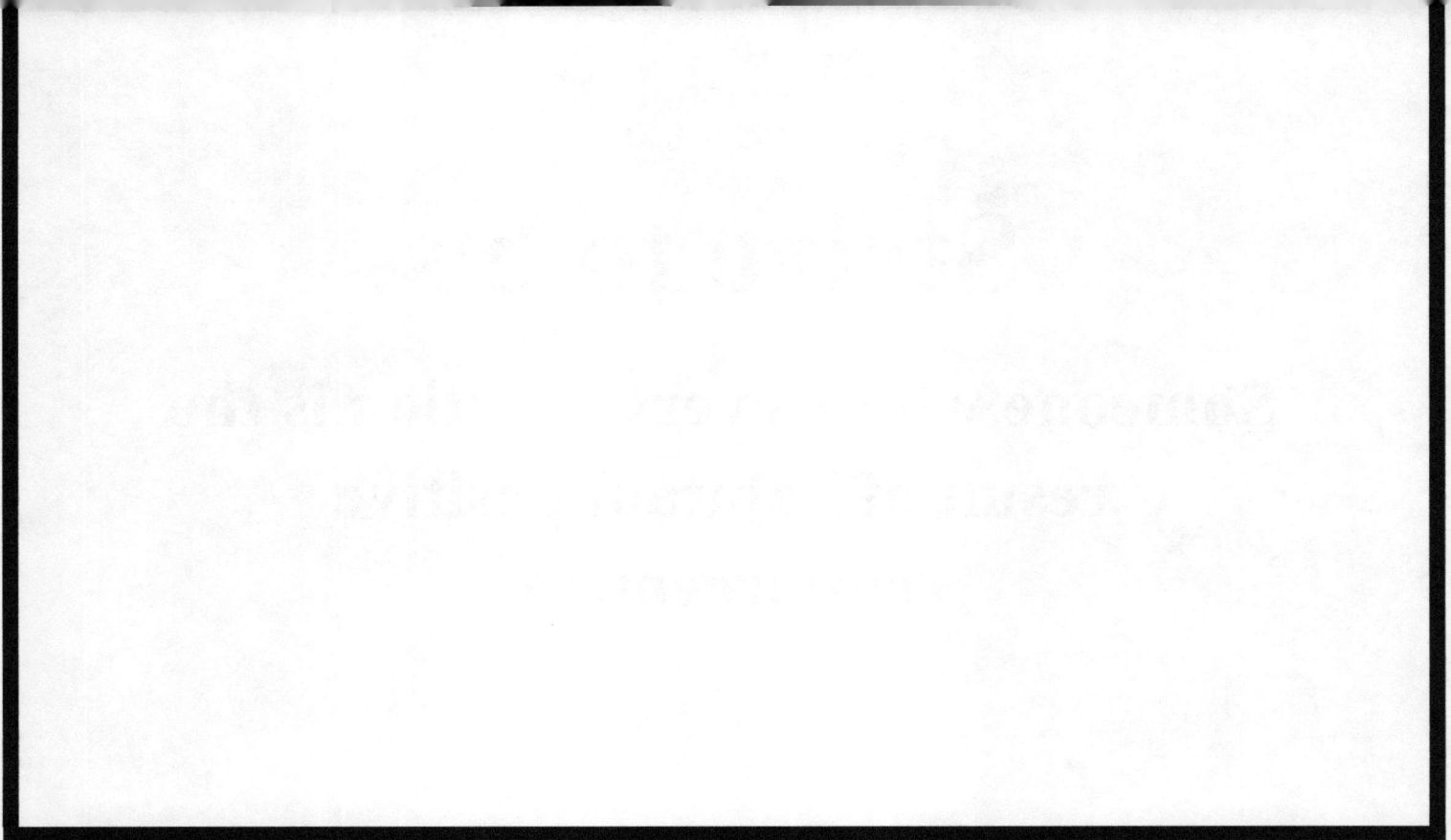

Strive to be

Someone who sees setback merely as a result of incomplete awareness.

Strive to be

Someone to whom pain and loss are catalysts for understanding and transcendence.

Strive to be

Someone who sees all challenges as opportunities for growth and improvement.

Strive to be

Someone who is happy for, and inspired and encouraged by, the success of others.

Strive to be

Someone who is known for and
inspired and encouraged by the
success of others.

Strive to be

Someone whose list of achievements has no omission based on fear, incompetence, or complacency.

Strive to be

Someone with an awareness that transcends your present situation, while being fully present

Strive to be

Someone who sees a reason for joy and appreciation in all situations.

Strive to be

Someone with the vision to see the structure, and thus the limits, of what others perceive only as obstacles.

Strive to be

Someone who understands competence regarding any endeavor to be a matter of conscious awareness and persistent, positive reinforcement.

Strive to be

Someone who sees creativity as your only limit.

Strive to be

Someone who realizes that fantasy is an actual aspect of reality and that it merely currently lacks the foundation required to exist in the physical realm.

Strive to be

Someone for whom solitude is the frequent occurrence of time spent with your best friend and trusted advisor.

Strive to be

Worthy of respect and trust in all manner of interaction.

Strive to be

Someone whose ability to oppose another, in any regard, is considered by all beings to be superior yet fair.

Strive to be

Someone whose ability to love and accept is not limited by fear, hatred, jealousy, or perspective.

Strive to be

Someone who has the courage to act rationally in all situations.

Strive to be

Someone who embodies balance at all times, in all situations.

Strive to be

Someone whose beliefs are eternally regarded by all honest, serious thinkers as properly conceived.

Strive to be

Someone who produces more environmentally beneficial resources than you consume.

Strive to be

Someone whose friendship and acquaintance is considered an honor by all who know of you.

Strive to be

Someone for whom every act of giving
is rooted in strength, not weakness.

Strive to be

Someone who can perceive of every possible existence and still desire your own.

STRIVE

www.ingramcontent.com/pod-product-compliance
Lightning Source LLC
La Vergne TN
LVHW091218080426
835509LV00009B/1060